Liz Doig is the owner and director of the boutique brand language consultancy, Wordtree.

Wordtree works in a number of ways. It helps organisations to develop and implement brand strategy. It also creates names, straplines and tone of voice. And it trains people to write – and helps global corporations to roll their tone of voice out across all their markets.

Liz is a brand consultant, writer and trainer. She has worked with organisations including Coutts, Standard Life, Budget Rent-a-Car, Durex, Intelligent Finance, as well as charities and public sector organisations.

She works with clients across the UK, Europe and North America in both English and French.

BRAND
LANGUAGE
TONE *of* VOICE
the WORDTREE WAY

LIZ DOIG

Wordtree & Me Limited

Published by Wordtree & Me Limited 2012
Copyright © Liz Doig 2012

Wordtree & Me Limited
Limited Reg NO: 7257996
www.wordtree.com

Studio One
127–129 Bute Street
Cardiff Bay
Cardiff, CF10 5LE
United Kingdom

A CIP record for this book is
available from the British Library.

Design by Ben Anslow
www.benanslow.com

ISBN NO: 978-0-9573873-0-0

With grateful thanks to the Wordtree team:

Jennifer Burns
Sandra Franklin
Matthew John
Caroline Godwin
and
Graeme Edwards

You're all superstars.

CONTENTS

INTRODUCTION

INTRODUCTION

AN INTRODUCTION *to* BRAND LANGUAGE

When I talk, whether I like it or not, I reveal a surprising amount about my personality.

We're not talking about accent here – we're talking about the words I use. And that's because my quirks of speech and the words I prefer and like the sound of – they're all a direct expression of who I am.

And because language is a two-way thing, something else happens when I talk. Everyone I speak to is making constant, and mostly subconscious judgements, about my personality and the relationship they think they're likely to have with me.

Am I someone they think they could get on with? Will I be useful to them? Do they feel equal to me? Inferior? Superior? Most of this processing is going on rapidly and subliminally.

So if someone answers the phone like this:

Hi, who am I speaking to?

You might already be forming an impression of the kind of person you are dealing with, and the kind of relationship you expect to have with them.

But if they answered the phone like this:

Good afternoon. May I inquire with whom I am speaking?

You'd be likely to form a different impression of them altogether.

The message didn't change in the slightest – but the choice of words tells us a huge amount about the person who wrote them or spoke them.

We're so attuned to the way people use language that we can usually identify a person simply from the words they use.

In Wordtree's tone of voice writing workshops, we often do an exercise where we get people to write in the voice of a famous person or character. We all spend a few minutes writing in the style of, say, Yoda or Homer Simpson. Then each person reads out what they've written and the rest of the group has to guess who they are.

It doesn't matter whether we run this exercise in London, Edinburgh or Montreal, the results are the same. Because the way we recognise personality isn't just about accent or the clothes someone is wearing – it's also about the words they use. Because the words so accurately express their personality, they can be reproduced and easily recognised.

SO WHAT DOES *this* HAVE TO DO WITH BRANDS?

In the not-too-distant past, all a brand had to do was tell you to buy into it. They may have supported their message with a persuading scientific fact:

Buy Zappo soap powder – scientifically proven to make whites whiter!

But the relationship was clear: Brands knew what was good for their consumers, and their consumers should jolly well listen and buy.

Now all that has changed. Consumers are savvier and more empowered than ever before. Brands and organisations can no longer tell consumers what to buy into – and quite right too.

Instead, the world's most successful brands have conversations with their consumers. They set out to be liked by them, not so much for what they do, but for who they are. Because once a consumer has decided that she or he has befriended a brand, they become loyal and keep the conversation going.

In this process, successful brands act like people rather than faceless, soulless corporations. And their consumers treat them like people too, embarking on a relationship with them.

This isn't so surprising. Every organisation I have ever worked with has its own character, its own way of doing things and its own way of viewing the world. This makes them not so very different from a person.

But brands need to beware. All the while they're having conversations with their consumers, their consumers are judging them by the words they use. Usually, this isn't even a conscious act – it's just what human beings are hardwired to do.

A brand's language has to be working really hard to give consumers the right subconscious cues – rather than accidentally sending out signals that it's going to be stuffy, difficult and unpleasant to deal with.

CREATING BRAND LANGUAGE

When you get a workforce together, every person will have their own style of writing and language use. Often it's one that has been drummed into them by the school, university or secretarial college they went to.

On top of that, different professions have their own ways of using language too. Lawyers, for example, use words in a very particular way. So do investment experts – and so do social workers and newspaper journalists. Every sector has its own – often fiercely guarded – style of communication.

Most workplaces have people from more than one profession in them. And they certainly contain people with different educational experiences, who've all been taught slightly different rules of English.

If a brand just lets everyone use their own style, consumers won't have a consistent personality to latch on to. The personality being conveyed will jump around depending on who's writing or answering the phone.

Which makes it more difficult for consumers to recognise a brand, to commit to a relationship with it and to trust it.

So increasingly, successful brands construct a style of language that must be used by everyone in the workforce, every time they communicate. Some organisations call this a tone of voice, others call it verbal identity and others still call it brand language.

Whatever it's called, its function has to be consistently conveying the personality of the brand, no matter who is writing or speaking.

Wordtree has created the tone of voice for several brands, from banks through to car rental firms, retailers and charities.

This textbook sets out the processes and devices we have developed to translate a brand's personality into a distinct and recognisable style of communication. We hope you find it useful.

HOW *to* USE THIS TEXTBOOK

We talk about "commercial writing" and "consumers" and "customers" throughout this book. But the content is relevant for anyone who wants their organisation to be able to communicate and persuade more effectively.

In a sense, every organisation – whether it's in the public, private or third sector, has "customers" – the people who consume or benefit from their services.

The structure of this textbook mirrors the stages of the process Wordtree has developed for designing and creating tone of voice. We call this Tone of Voice the Wordtree Way.

The strategic sections – where you map out territories and define the personality of your brand – are relevant, no matter which language you're working in.

The rest of this textbook is geared very much towards the English language. Who knows? In the future we may publish editions for other languages. For now though, English it is.

HOW *to* USE THIS TEXTBOOK

Each section is followed by exercises that
have been designed to help you create a style
of language that is right for your own brand
or organisation.

And because we know that nothing brings
ideas and theories to life more than
examples, we've invented a brand called
Lil & Jasper's. You'll come across our
made-up brand all the way through the book.

We've used it throughout to illustrate the
process we use when we create a tone of voice
for a new client.

HOW *to* USE THIS TEXTBOOK

Please scribble on the pages of this book as you go along. For some exercises you'll need a notebook as well. The important thing is to get your ideas down on the page – even if you're not sure they're completely right.

Recording your thoughts, ideas and doodles is all part of the process.

Hopefully, you're itching to start now. So how about you pick up a pencil and we'll get working on your brand's language.

>>>

INTRODUCING LIL & JASPER'S

INTRODUCING LIL & JASPER'S

INTRODUCING LIL & JASPER'S

When we're running brand language workshops, we find the best way to bring theories to life is to show them at work in examples.

And we thought the most straightforward way to show a running example all the way through this book would be to invent a brand. So we have.

You won't find Lil & Jasper's on the shelves of any store. But you'll get to know this fictitious brand quite well through the pages of this book. We'll be using it to show you how our processes work and to help you see the kinds of decisions we make when we're working with real brands.

The made-up world of Lil & Jasper's

Lil & Jasper's is a frozen pizza brand with a difference. It tastes amazing *and* it's healthy and convenient. We've given it a whole back story too.

Lil and Jasper were childhood sweethearts who eventually got married and opened a deli in the city where they grew up – Portland, Oregon, USA.

They're passionate about good food, but they're pretty cool and laid-back characters too. They enjoy their life, but they realise how busy people have become. So they've taken some of their favourite recipes and turned them into healthy convenience food. Because they don't think convenience food has to mean junk food.

So no matter how busy you are, you can always eat well if you've got a Lil & Jasper's pizza in the freezer. Lil & Jasper's is available in traditional formats and also in smaller, individual rectangular servings, just like in the deli.

THE LIL & JASPER'S BRAND

When brands and organisations begin to think about marketing themselves more widely, it helps a lot if they adopt a systematic approach.

This means setting down in stone what they do, what they believe in, how they do it and what kind of organisation they are. Typically, brands document their values, their credentials and the way they do business.

To be able to understand a brand's personality and to create its tone of voice, we need to know this information. We've decided Lil & Jasper's has these values and credentials.

VALUES	WHY SHOULD ANYONE BUY THEIR PRODUCTS?
Stylish simplicity • Fresh and thoughtful **Creativity** • Rooted in a passion for making things taste and look great • Curious, imaginative and open to new ideas	**Great food from people who understand you're busy** • Using organic, ethically sourced ingredients • No added salt, preservatives, hydrogenated oil or high-fructose corn syrup

And as you've seen, we've also decided what Lil & Jasper's looks like.

In reality, if we were working on the development of a new brand identity for Lil & Jasper's, we'd develop the brand platform first – which would contain information like the brand's values and credentials. And then we'd work on the language while a design agency interpreted the brand visually.

But to help us show you our process for creating a tone of voice, we just went ahead and asked a designer to create a basic visual identity for Lil & Jasper's.

Anyway, first things first. Before we even start developing a tone of voice for real or made-up brands, we need to look at the basics of good commercial writing.

GOOD COMMERCIAL WRITING

GOOD COMMERCIAL WRITING

GOOD COMMERCIAL WRITING

Before we even get into the business of tone of voice, we need to get to grips with an important idea – that commercial writing is different.

If you're reading this book, the chances are you use words to persuade people to change their behaviour or buy into something different.

You may want them to read a poster and decide to stop smoking. Or you may want them to pick up the phone and order a new kitchen from you after they've read your brochure or website.

Whatever you want to persuade people to do, you'll have a greater chance of success if you get your head around two important things:

• Commercial writing is not like writing a university essay
• And most of the time, people don't want to read it

The first idea might seem like a strange thing to say. But a lot of very highly qualified and educated people struggle to write well for commercial audiences, because they're still trying to write university essays.

Commercial writing is not about showcasing your intelligence. In fact, it's got very little to do with you at all. It's more about conveying information rapidly, pleasingly and interestingly. We often describe it as *transacting information.*

As a commercial communicator, you should want the transaction to happen swiftly and smoothly. You have an idea in your head that you want to get into your reader's head. And you should want there to be as few barriers as possible to this transfer happening.

Your writing should be understood the first time it's read. Because if a reader has to go back and re-read a sentence, it just isn't working hard enough.

And that other notion – that people don't want to read the majority of commercial copy – can come as a bit of a shocker too.

But the thing is, we live in an age of information. The stuff is absolutely everywhere – and the way most of us deal with this overload of words and messages is to ignore practically all of it.

Commercial writing has to be pretty good to even grab the reader's attention in the first place. And bloody marvellous to keep them reading.

What follows is a list of things you need to get sorted even before you start to apply tone of voice.

It's a roundup of the most common mistakes we see people make when they write for commercial audiences – as well as suggestions for fixing them.

GET *to the* POINT

>>>

People who are really good at writing things like university essays and scientific reports can become frustrated when the approach doesn't work commercially.

They think, "But I set out my stall. I explained that my company is expert in offering financial advice and that we've been doing it for more than 15 years. I told them where we'd got our qualifications and that we're local and that we can come to them. So why has no-one responded to my ad?"

There could be a number of things going on with this scenario. But the most likely are that:

a) they wrote too much
b) they didn't get to the point, *from the perspective of the reader*

In a university essay or a report, it's normal to set out an argument, develop it, and then come to the conclusion.

In commercial writing, you need to flip that idea on its head and get to the point straight away. Most commercial readers will only give your writing a quick glance, and if they don't see anything interesting immediately, you'll lose them.

Commercial readers owe you nothing, and you cannot force them to read a single word you've written. Instead, you need to waste as little of their time as you possibly can by clearly setting out what you do and why it's relevant to them.

EXAMPLE

DOESN'T GET TO THE POINT	GETS TO THE POINT
Offering you the benefit of more than 15 years' experience When Frank Wilson left university with a First Class Degree in Finance, he had only one wish – to work in his local community. Now, 15 years later, Wilson Financial Services (WFS) helps hundreds of families and local businesses across Staffordshire plan effectively for the future. We are committed to delivering the most professional service and can accommodate you in our own offices, or visit you in your own home or business environment. For more information or to make an appointment, please call 0800 000 000. You can also find out more about us on our website: www.wfs-staffordshire.co.uk or by emailing us at inquiries@wfs-staffs.co.uk	**Expert financial advice on your doorstep** • Savings and pensions • Mortgages • Tax planning We can visit you at home, in your office – or you can come and see us. **Call 0800 000 000** inquiries@wfs-staffs.co.uk www.wfs-staffordshire.co.uk *Wilson Financial Services – serving Staffordshire since 1996.*

In the first version, there is just too much going on. The author hasn't got to the point from the perspective of the reader. When the reader is browsing their local paper, they're at the point when all they want to know is what you do, where you do it, and how to make contact. In the second version, the reader can see these points in less than a second.

<<<

SENTENCE LENGTHS

Long sentences that are crammed with messages are hard to read and digest. The reader is just being asked to hold onto too much information and the process rapidly becomes exhausting. And an exhausted reader is a bored reader.

So as a rule of thumb, you should be able to read any sentence you've written out loud in one breath. Generally, sentences shouldn't be more than 25 words long.

So strip out any words that absolutely don't need to be there.

Also, try to limit yourself to two messages per sentence. This means you shouldn't be trying to say more than two things in one sentence.

If we restrict ourselves to one or two messages per sentence, we don't compromise the amount of detail we can convey – we just deliver it in a much more rapid and fluid way.

Tip

If you're struggling to trim your text down to the bare essentials, just ask yourself, "What does the reader want from this communication?"

Be honest. Commercial readers just don't have the time to pore over your text to see if there's anything remotely interesting in it for them.

EXAMPLE

LONG SENTENCES CONTAINING LOTS OF MESSAGES	SHORTER SENTENCES – MORE EFFECTIVE COMMUNICATION
We are passionate about enabling customers to focus on their strengths, confident in the knowledge that their IT systems will reliably support them and their colleagues in their business pursuits. If you are serious about getting value from your current IT systems, or you're looking for ways to keep your business ahead of the competition, you will be amazed at how we can help.	We look after your IT systems so you can get on with what you do best. We'll help you get the most from your systems – and we'll keep you ahead of the competition.

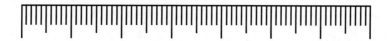

Shorter sentences certainly make messages easier to digest. They have another interesting effect too – they convey confidence.

A short sentence says, "I know what I'm talking about." Lengthier sentences can make you sound unsure and waffly.

Tip

Read what you've written back out loud to yourself. If you can't read your sentences out loud in one breath, chop them into smaller units – and get rid of every single word that absolutely doesn't need to be there.

SHORT WORDS

English is a beautiful language. And because of its mixed heritage, we often have more than one word for the same concept. Often, one will be a longer word with Latin roots and the other will be a shorter word with Anglo-Saxon roots.

Educated people have usually been through education systems that reward them for using the longer, Latinate versions.

While it's great to have a wide vocabulary, it's important to remember that to transact information, shorter words are often highly effective.

SPEED

Short words allow you to convey more energy and pace in your writing. The reader gallops through sentences constructed of short words, and this gives him or her the impression that what they're reading is easy. This is why publications like The Economist and the Financial Times use a surprising number of shorter words.

EMOTION

If English is our first language, we tend to learn the short words first. So children can generally say "get" and "need" before they learn "acquire" and "require". Which means the short words become our instinctive words – our default vocabulary, if you like. They're the ones we use if we're in any way emotional. And this makes them powerful in commercial communications, because they feel more emotive and genuine to readers.

CONFIDENCE *and* AUTHORITY

Shorter words convey confidence and authority. A publication like The Economist uses longer words sparingly – rarely having them make up more than 25% of a sentence. Yet we don't read the Economist and think it lacks authority. The effect is quite the opposite. We read about complex world affairs quickly and enjoyably, and we come away from the experience feeling more informed. That is entirely down to the skill of The Economist's writers.

EXAMPLE

DON'T JUST AUTOMATICALLY USE THESE WORDS	ALLOW YOURSELF TO USE THESE WORDS TOO
LOCATION	*PLACE*
ACQUIRE	*GET*
REQUIRE	*NEED*
DONATE	*GIVE*
ASCERTAIN	*FIND OUT*
DEMAND	*ASK*
PURCHASE	*BUY*

Tip

Don't feel you have to dress your words up. Simple can be elegant and beautiful. Remember commercial writing isn't about you, or showcasing your intelligence. It's about transacting information rapidly and effectively – and short words can help you achieve this.

PREFER VERBS

Human brains find it hard to retain lists of nouns. That's why children's games like *I went to market and I bought…* are a challenge. There quickly comes a point where your brain says, "Nope, I can't take any more."

As commercial writers, it therefore doesn't make sense to put too many nouns into a sentence. If we do, we know that we're just making it harder for the reader.

In formal English and business speak, verbs are often replaced by nouns – which tends to increase the word count, as well as making the reader work harder to process the information.

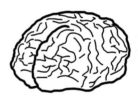

EXAMPLE

FIVE NOUNS – SO THE SENTENCE IS HARDER TO GRASP	FIVE NOUNS HAVE BECOME ONE, AND THE INFORMATION IS TRANSACTED MORE RAPIDLY
In order to deliver an optimal interactive experience, we have made maximum use of digital solutions comprising our blog and Twitter channels.	To make the experience as interactive as possible, we're blogging and tweeting.

Tip

Allow yourself to write more like you would speak at home. Would you ever get in after work and say to your partner, "Darling! In order to deliver an optimal dinner experience, I've made maximum use of our microwave solution?" Probably not, so there's no need to do it in your commercial writing either.

AVOID REPETITION

AVOID REPETITION

AVOID REPETITION

AVOID REPETITION

AVOID REPETITION

AVOID REPETITION

AVOID REPETITION

If you know someone who tells you the same stories over and over again, you begin to want to hide when you see them coming. We don't like repetition. It bores us.

We want our writing to be interesting to readers, so we need to keep it fresh and varied. Which means we need to avoid using the same words in a communication.

>>>

EXAMPLE

REPETITIVE AND DULL	FRESHER AND MORE ENTERTAINING
Delicious treats and snacks for dogs At Poochies Pet Parlour, we have a delicious range of freshly baked treats and snacks for dogs of all sizes. Our treats and snacks have all been baked especially for the dog in your life. They don't contain any nasties that will upset dogs. With Poochies range of delicious treats and snacks for dogs, your dog will have a wagging tail all day!	**Waggy tails all round** Poochies treats and snacks are freshly baked every day using recipes that will keep your doggie bouncing with health.

Tip

Don't repeat your headline in the first sentence. You know you may only have split seconds to convince your audience to carry on reading – so don't blow it with repetition from the word go.

EXCLAMATION MARKS

>>>

There are two groups of writers who use a lot of exclamation marks. One of them is teenage girls. The other is authors who want to convince you they're being friendly.

In commercial writing, exclamation marks are not your friends. It's unlikely that you'll want to sound like a teenage girl (though if you do – go for your life and sprinkle them like confetti – and add smiley faces while you're at it).

It is possible to sound friendly, grown-up *and* confident at the same time. But only if you lose the exclamation marks. So sweep them up and put them in the bin.

EXAMPLE

DID A 13-YEAR-OLD WRITE THIS?	THIS SOUNDS MORE GROWN-UP AND LESS CHEAP
We're offering you a whole 20% off!!	**We're offering you a whole 20% off**
It's our biggest sale yet this year! Save on all our latest ranges! Stock up on the treats you love!	It's our biggest sale of the year. So save on all our latest ranges and stock up on the treats you love.
Go on, you deserve it!!!!	Go on, you deserve it.

Tip

If you know you have an exclamation mark habit, do try to cut down. Allow yourself just one per communication. Only one. Then you'll have to choose very carefully where you put it. Before you know it, you'll see that all your sentences stand up perfectly well without the manically happy punctuation at the end.

ACTIVE *and* PASSIVE VOICES

In English, we have two ways of expressing verbs. We're not talking about tense – which is *when* the action happens. The active and passive voices are more about *who* is doing the action.

Often with the passive voice, you don't know who is doing the doing. Because of this, it can make communications feel dispassionate and uninvolved. There is no emotion when we use the passive voice – which is why police officers often use it.

Both the active and the passive voice have their uses in commercial writing.

The majority of times, it's most helpful to use the active voice, because it helps to reinforce relationships between organisations and their consumers.

When you use the passive voice, you create an unemotional space between yourself and the reader – and this can make it useful if you're responding to complaint letters, for example.

The trick is to judge carefully when you use the active or the passive voice, and not to just plump for the passive because you think that's what business communications should do.

EXAMPLE

		EFFECT ON READER
PASSIVE	You will be charged £125 for refuelling if your hire car is returned with an empty tank.	The communication is entirely dispassionate. The reader doesn't know who will make the charge – and the message feels aloof and slightly dishonest as a result.
ACTIVE	If you bring your hire car back with an empty fuel tank, we'll charge you £125 for a refill.	Now the reader knows exactly who makes the charge – and the communication feels more up-front and honest.

Tip

Writers sometimes opt for the passive when they feel uncomfortable about what they're writing. In the car hire example, it's quite possible that the author of the passive version didn't like what they were writing – so they pushed it away from themselves by using the passive voice. It's like saying, "It's not me doing this, honest. It's just the faceless organisation I work for." Try to be really brave and not do this. It's usually much fairer and more helpful for the reader if you use the active voice.

JARGON

Every sector, every profession and every activity has a set of vocabulary associated with it. So if you go to a photography club you might know all about f-stops and exposures. If your passion is mountaineering, you'll know your belays from your biners. And if you work in marketing, you'll be able to have perfectly sensible conversations with your colleagues about hierarchies and touchpoints and the like.

Jargon gets a bad rap in most writing guides which tell you to avoid it, point blank. We kind of think it can have its uses, if your audience understands it.

The problem with jargon is that it's insidious stuff. You start using it and before you know it you've forgotten that it's not normal vocabulary, and that other people might not get it. Even worse, they might think they get it, but have a completely different understanding of your terms and acronyms.

So the advice we always give in our workshops is if you're talking to end consumers, you need to stick to the kind of language you'd use at home. If you're talking to a B2B audience who'll know what your terminology means, then it would be silly to paraphrase. Just don't wallow in it.

BUSINESS SPEAK

Now this is a whole other world of weird vocabulary. Sometime in the early 90s, perfectly normal office workers started to speak a new lingo. They got rid of verbs like "to do" and replaced them with "deliver". They no longer talked about "problems" or "issues" but started calling the bad stuff "challenges".

This language probably came out of MBA classrooms and then spread to whole workforces.

There are two problems with using business speak in commercial communications:

1. It sounds silly – especially to people who've never had the joys of working in a corporate environment
2. It strips emotion out of communications – which can be handy in meeting rooms, but makes connecting with commercial audiences very difficult

All the following pieces of language may be understood in a meeting room (though don't bet your last fiver on it), but don't let them land on the page – even if you're involved in B2B writing.

"

GET YOUR DUCKS IN A ROW

DELIVERING

BOILING THE OCEANS

LOW-HANGING FRUIT

HELICOPTER VIEWS

360 FEEDBACK

"

We're sure you can think of hundreds more.

BREAK *the* RULES

If you've been reading through this book tut-tutting because your English teacher said you shouldn't start a sentence with a conjunction – or leave a preposition hanging – then this section is just for you.

Our English teachers taught us a lot of good stuff. And hopefully, they fired a passion for the written word.

What a lot of high school English teaching does too, however, is pass on rules that were gifted to us by the Victorians.

Middle class Victorians were an interesting group of people. When the establishment sneered at their new money, they thumbed their nose back and simply became the establishment. They changed society and they changed the world.

One of their many, many legacies has been their "rules" about correct use of the English language.

STARTING SENTENCES *with* CONJUNCTIONS

Before the Victorians, starting a sentence with a conjunction was an acceptable thing to do. Just open a King James Bible and have a look at the first page of Genesis.

But after the Victorians, this was deemed to be "vulgar". And that, quite simply, seems to have been the only justification for this particular rule. (Many of the other rules the Victorians concocted were based on Latin – but you can't even blame Latin for this one.)

Starting a sentence with a conjunction adds punch and pace to a piece of writing. It's particularly handy if you have a long sentence that you need to break up.

HANGING PREPOSITIONS

Some English teachers didn't like us leaving prepositions dangling at the end of a sentence.

So we may have become very skilful at wrapping sentences up into neat little parcels with the prepositions all tucked up cosily inside.

Churchill called this rule, "...arrant pedantry, up with which I will not put".

The problem with parcelled-up preps is that they can make sentences overly long and complicated.

"This is the woman I've been talking to."

Becomes,

"This is the woman with whom I've been talking."

Parcelling up prepositions can make sentences overly wordy – which isn't ideal in commercial writing.

Again, just allow yourself to write more like you'd speak.

CONTRACTIONS

These are when you take two words and push them together to make one. An apostrophe is used to show were letters have been lost to make the contracted word.

do not – **don't**
will not – **won't**

They're disliked by a lot of English teachers. Well, they dislike some of them. They're not too bothered about us contracting "of the clock" to "o'clock" and most have no problems with poetic contractions like "o'er hill and dale".

But we may have been told in school not to use contractions like "we're" or "you're".

Contractions can make a sentence flow more easily though – so don't dismiss them out of hand. Used sparingly, they can make a potentially forbidding piece of text easier to get through.

It can be useful to remember why our teachers expended so much red ink enforcing these "rules".

From the ages of five through to 16, kids might gabble, learn their own schoolyard lingo or stick with the handful of words they know will get them by.

Largely, our teachers wanted us to develop the linguistic skills that will give us the best chances in life.

GOOD COMMERCIAL LANGUAGE

So they might have told you never to use a word like "nice" or "got" or "put". That doesn't mean those words are invalid. It just means they wanted us to learn more than the basics.

And if they told you not to use contractions, maybe it was because they didn't want you to *only* use contractions.

The thing is, we're all grown-ups now. So we can bend and flex our language in the ways we need to transact information with our readers.

Think of the language you work with as a raw material – like clay. You don't have to make classical vases out of the clay every time. You can make anything from a brick to avant garde sculptures with it. Because you're in charge of the words – they're not in charge of you.

GOOD COMMERCIAL LANGUAGE

So this is your starting point, your foundation. Whenever your text feels flat or less than sparkling, use this check list:

- Am I getting to the point?
- Are my sentences too long?
- Am I using too much fancy vocabulary?
- Are there too many nouns in my sentences?
- What happens if I flip from the passive to the active voice?
- Will my audience understand any jargon I've used?
- Have I used business speak?
- What would happen if I broke some of the rules?

If all you do to your writing is use this list, the odds are that your communications will improve drastically. You'll have interesting, relevant writing that's immediately understandable.

What we're going to do next is look at how we take these good foundations and overlay them with personality.

MAP OUT WHERE YOUR BRAND LANGUAGE FITS

MAP OUT WHERE YOUR BRAND
LANGUAGE FITS

MAP OUT *how* YOUR BRAND'S
LANGUAGE *fits* INTO A *wider* LANDSCAPE

Whenever we start to work with a new client, we carry out an audit of the sector they operate in.

We get samples of writing from their direct competitors. We may also look at products and services that are related to our client's work.

So for example, if we were working with a high-end law firm that prided itself on individual service and industry-defining knowledge, we might also consider the ways that organisations like private banks, tax consultancies and investment houses use words.

Typically, we go through web pages, contracts, brochures, packaging, manuals, training materials, tweets – and any other written materials we can get our hands on.

Then we use checklists like this to analyse the language each competitor is using:

+ When you hear this brand's words spoken out loud, what kind of person does it sound like?
+ Do you want to hear more?
+ Are you bored?
+ Does the brand speak mostly in the active or passive voice?

+ How long are the sentences it uses?
+ Does it use mostly verbs or nouns in a sentence?
+ Does it use long words or short words?
+ Does it use jargon or business speak?

Usually, sectors are characterised by maybe two or three dominant styles. Or sometimes it's more like there's a spectrum between one style and another.

THE FROZEN PIZZA LANDSCAPE

When we began to create the brand language for our pizza brand, one of our first jobs was to go shopping.

We hit the supermarkets to find brands that are already operating in the frozen pizza sector.

We also know that Lil & Jasper's has a farmer's market feel to it. So if we saw products with a similar look and feel, we popped those in our trolley too.

We don't just go to one or two supermarkets.

We know Lil & Jasper's needs to have an up-market feel – so we made sure we visited Waitrose and the Harvey Nicks Food Hall – and any real life farmer's markets we can get to.

Then we bring our haul back to the studio and keep all the packaging.

(The pizza doesn't go to waste either – we're a hungry bunch.)

Then we audit the language that's being used by each brand.

And finally, our notes and scribbles are tidied up into a chart a bit like this one.

>>>

LANGUAGE *in the* FROZEN PIZZA SECTOR

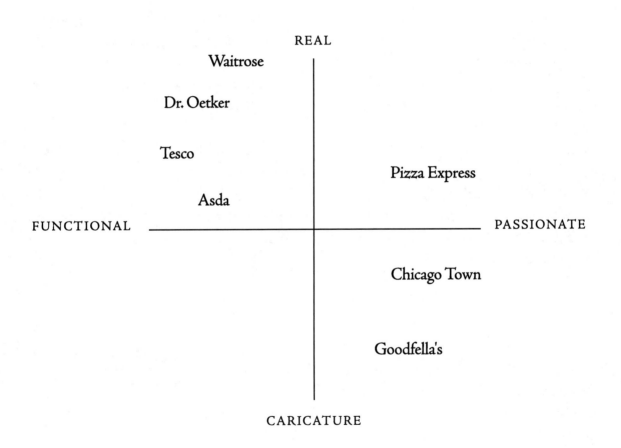

When we analysed language in the frozen pizza sector, what we found was a space where brands either sound functional and convenient – or they borrowed heavily from native or second generation Italian speech patterns and stereotypes.

So supermarket own brands and Dr Oetker tend toward the functional end of the spectrum, while Goodfella's, Chicago Town and Pizza Express talk in fiery, short sentences to convey passion and fast action. On top of that, the first two use a stylised, ba-da-bing language that conveys the kind of Italian-American fast talk that most consumers will have seen in films.

The big question was did Lil & Jasper's fit into this landscape – or did it want to create its own territory?

DIFFERENTIATION *or* "ME TOO"?

As you're building or reviewing your brand, you need to ask an important question: Do you want to look and sound the same as everyone else in your sector? Or do you want to stand out and feel different?

Every sector tends to have its own look and feel. They have their own signature styles of language too.

For example, you'd be surprised if you walked into a garage to get your car serviced and it was painted fresh pastel pinks, had a fuchsia logo and gave you a receipt that read: *Your naughty little clutch has cost you £150, but don't worry, we've put a nice sensible one in there for you now.*

We're surprised, because this isn't the sort of language we'd expect to get from a garage.

Mapping out how your competitors speak gives you an overview of the norms for your sector.

But you then have to decide – Do you want to play it the same as everyone else – or do something different?

Me too
Many brands start off trying to look and sound the same as others in their sector. Then a few years down the line when they've become more established, they find they need to make more of an effort to allow their personality to shine through. Because otherwise, it's very hard to show why they're different and better than their competitors.

Differentiating from the outset takes guts – and often, a heap of money to invest in brand development and marketing.

Disrupting the marketplace
Making the decision to stand out is a brave thing to do – but it can be highly effective and profitable too.

For example, twenty years ago, who would have thought that a new airline would launch with orange livery and a more down-to-earth proposition – and change the way we all travel?

You just have to decide – do you find a place to snuggle in amongst your competitors, or do you stake out completely new territory?

So what should Lil & Jasper's do?
The landscape for our healthy frozen pizza brand is dominated by language that's either functional and convenient – which just doesn't feel high-end enough for Lil & Jasper's. Or it's passionate and Italian. And that isn't right for Lil & Jasper's either. This is a brand that came out of a deli in Portland, Oregon.

So the answer to the question for Lil & Jasper's has to be differentiation.

To get a better idea of how different, we analysed the language used across related foodie and nutritionally-conscious brands.

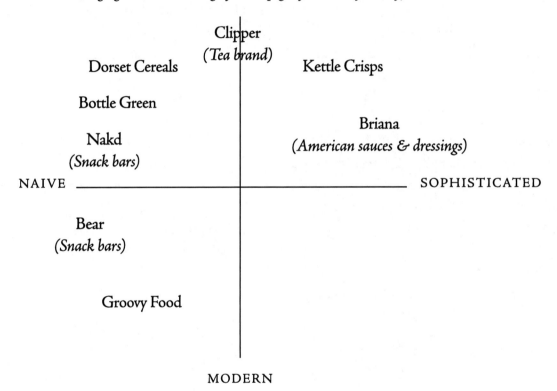

1950s-STYLE GUSTO

(language sounds like it's straight from the pages of an Enid Blyton story)

Clipper
(Tea brand)

Dorset Cereals

Kettle Crisps

Bottle Green

Briana
(American sauces & dressings)

Nakd
(Snack bars)

NAIVE ⸺⸺⸺⸺⸺⸺⸺⸺⸺⸺ SOPHISTICATED

Bear
(Snack bars)

Groovy Food

MODERN

DIFFERENTIATION *or* "ME TOO"?

And this is where things got interesting. Communications in foodie land were largely conveyed in an innocent, child-like style – or in a very earnest head girl style that sounded like it had been written by Enid Blyton. We found the sector to be full of fun and friendly childish or nostalgic voices.

Which left an interesting and unoccupied space for Lil & Jasper's. It's the one that's still blank on the chart – the quadrant between modern and sophisticated. Which coincides very nicely with the grown-up, simple and relevant food choice that Lil & Jasper's wants to be.

MAP OUT YOUR TERRITORY – EXERCISES

1. Go shopping
Make a list of your competitors and get samples of the way they use words.

If your brand is a consumable like a frozen pizza, this can be as simple as jumping in the car and visiting supermarkets.

If your brand is a specialist service, hit Google to find out who your competitors are. Then sign up for their newsletters and send off for their brochures.

If you want to open a café, go exploring in your neighbourhood. Visit other cafés and take their napkins and paper cups, take photos of their interiors if you can, make a note of how they phrase their menus and customer communications both on site and online.

Let your friends, relatives and colleagues know that you need examples of packaging, brochures, tender documents… whatever you can get your hands on.

2. Analyse
Take your samples and make detailed notes about the kinds of language your competitors and related brands are using.

Use a checklist like this >>>

If you shut your eyes and hear this brand's words spoken out loud, what kind of person does it sound like? If a real person springs to mind, use a photo of them too.	
Do you want to hear more?	
Are you bored?	
Does the brand speak mostly in the active or passive voice?	
How long are the sentences it uses?	
Does it use mostly verbs or nouns in a sentence?	
Does it use long words or short words?	
Does it use jargon or business speak?	
Does it tell you stories?	

When we're doing this, we use separate sheets of A4 white paper, which allows us to doodle, and also to sketch the results out across our workshop table.

We might even attach a photo of a person the writing style reminds us of. We thought the voice of Goodfella's pizza sounded like Robert De Niro in The Untouchables, so we clipped a picture of him to the Goodfella's audit.

3. Categorise

You tend to find that there are maybe two, three or four styles in each sector.

Your job now is to give each of the styles you find a name. In the frozen pizza category, there were two styles:

Functional and Italian

And within those two, there was a feeling that some styles were more manufactured than others. That's why we ended up with the quadrants going from left to right, functional through to passionate. Then from top to bottom, real and caricature.

In the related brands, the styles were different
– ranging from naïve and whimsical through
to sophisticated. The vertical axis marked a
range in styles from modern, through to
lashings of ginger beer-style 1950s language.

**4. Map out the language styles of your
competitors on a chart**
Group the different styles you've found into
categories and plot them out on a chart.

Turn over for chart >>>

LANGUAGE *in* YOUR SECTOR

MAP OUT YOUR TERRITORY – EXERCISES

When you've identified the types of language that are being used in your sector, jot them down on the graph. Then place all your competitors on it, depending on the type of language they use.

In our experience, this shape of graph works well for many sectors, but it might not be quite right for yours. So do feel free to adapt it.

5. Decide if you're going to differentiate
Is your language going to be like others in your sector? Or are you going to do something completely different?

You can use your chart to decide where you need to be.

If you want to differentiate, look for clear space. That means looking for an area of the chart that no-one else is occupying.

Once you decide where your brand fits, you can then begin to define its personality.

>>>

DEFINE YOUR BRAND'S PERSONALITY

DEFINE YOUR BRAND'S PERSONALITY

DEFINE YOUR BRAND'S PERSONALITY

What is your brand's personality?
And what kind of relationship do you want to have with your audiences?

At the beginning of this book we said that tone of voice is personality expressed in words. And that's true.

Successful brands – to a large extent – act like people. They make plans and decisions based on a set of beliefs or values. They have goals in life, and rules of conduct to guide the way they achieve them.

They give you a consistently clear sense of what they do, how they're going to do it, and what they're going to be like to deal with. And this allows you, as a consumer, to decide whether you want to form a relationship with them, based on a reasonable expectation of what it will be like.

When you deal with IKEA, for example, you're probably expecting friendliness and a creative, can-do approach. In fact, you might be very disappointed if you don't get that.

Yet if you deal with a budget airline, you might expect a different relationship where you're prepared to accept a no-frills relationship that often dispenses with courtesy.

In the same way, you'd be surprised if Microsoft tried to go all funky and down with the kids. You'd probably be a little distrustful of them if they did.

Successful brands communicate in ways that consistently express their personalities.

Because brand language is rooted in personality, the first step to creating a tone of voice is to think long and hard about what your brand's personality really is.

We often come across tone of voice guidelines that are unhelpfully vague. They'll tell you that the writing needs to be "friendly" and "accessible". But there are many, many ways of being friendly, ranging from formal but agreeable, all the way through to matey and over-familiar.

To create a tone that's right for your brand, you need to be more precise. If your brand is friendly, what kind of friendly do you mean? If it's professional, what kind of professional? Stuffy and old school? Or technically proficient? Or do you just mean someone who'd wear a tie to work rather than a T-shirt?

Be true

When you're writing down words to describe the personality of your brand, keep it real.

If your organisation is staid and traditional, it's no good trying to make it something it's not.

You'll just end up seeming like a middle-aged man trying to dance the Lambada at a family wedding. He thinks he's strutting his stuff just fine, but everyone watching is thinking, "Ah, middle-aged man having a moment." They know his true self is most at home in an armchair listening to Gardeners' Question Time.

Your brand's words need to fit. They need to feel right. And that's only going to happen if you're honest about your personality.

YOU NEED *to* ASK YOURSELF ALL KINDS *of* QUESTIONS

- What kind of clothes would your brand wear?

- What would it do in its spare time?

- What kind of newspapers would it read?

- Which TV shows or films would it watch?

- Would you be friends with your brand? Or would you look up to it? Or go to it in times of crisis for reliable and trustworthy support?

- If you wrote a lonely hearts ad for your brand, how would you describe it and what would it be looking for?

Tip

It's often useful to say what your brand isn't, as well as what it is. For example, Brand X is professionally friendly. It's not aloof and stand-offish – and it certainly isn't matey either.

Be consistent

Remember that for the successful brands – the IKEAs, Googles and Apples; it doesn't matter how many divisions or departments they're made up of. They always write and talk in the same way, consistently conveying the same personality. And that's a large part of what allows their consumers to bond so powerfully with them.

And because consumers expect to have conversations and direct interactions with brands, communicating in a consistent voice is really important. If your brand doesn't, you are diminishing its ability to form relationships with your audiences.

Tip

Inconsistency puts consumers off, because they don't know what they're dealing with. So you should use a consistent style of language across your marketing materials, your terms and conditions, your receipts and invoices or your contracts for new employees. Every piece of written communication is an opportunity to reinforce your brand.

And what if the personality of the brand you're working with has already been defined?

If you're working with a brand that has already defined its personality, you could skip this step altogether.

However it could be worth checking that the existing information gives you enough to go on.

We've seen many descriptions of brand personality that either just say "friendly and accessible" – or they set out an unhelpfully long list of words.

To be able to create a tone of voice, you need a better handle on a brand's personality than this – so just go ahead and define it yourself.

A note on brand values and personality

Other brands will point to their values and tell you to work from them. But values are not a description of personality.

Two people can share the same values. They may both think, for example, that it's morally wrong to avoid paying tax. They may also think that it's a good idea to give money to charities every month.

But that doesn't mean they'll have the same personalities. One could be a fusspot control freak who stresses over details and never leaves the house in clothes that haven't been recently dry cleaned. The other could be so laid-back their house is a tip and they can't remember to keep appointments.

These people will communicate in different ways and you would relate to them differently, because despite the shared values, they have very different personalities. And it's the personality that drives the communication style – not the values.

So how are we going to define the personality of Lil & Jasper's?

>>>

LIL & JASPER'S PERSONALITY

Our healthy pizza brand is an invention – but then, so are a lot of brands. Some come with a real back story, others have to make them up. In our made-up healthy pizza land, Lil and Jasper are childhood sweethearts who got married and decided to turn their passion for food into a career. They opened their deli in Portland, Oregon and word soon spread around the neighbourhood that their food was healthy, delicious and convenient.

So they came up with the idea of making healthy deliciousness even more convenient and launched their frozen pizza range.

We know this much about Lil & Jasper's – but you can be healthy, delicious and convenient in a huge number of ways. So let's find out more about the personality of Lil & Jasper's.

1. What kind of clothes would Lil & Jasper's wear?

They'd probably wear understated designer clothes with bits and pieces they've picked up in both chain stores and vintage boutiques. Nothing too fussy – frayed Jil Sander jeans and a pair of Havaianas would suit Lil & Jasper's just fine. The brand wouldn't be seen dead in cheesecloth. It's not a hippy. It's stylish and world-aware.

2. What would Lil & Jasper's do in its spare time?

Probably catch a show or a bit of arthouse cinema. It might check out farmer's markets. Or cook dinner for friends. Lil & Jasper's likes getting creative and doing things like writing and upcycling. Lil & Jasper's enjoys travel too.

3. What kind of newspapers would Lil & Jasper's read? Or which films or TV shows would it watch?

Lil & Jasper's gets most of its information online, but it might pick up a New York Times every now and again. It's not big on TV, but it does listen to underground radio stations.

So let's use this information to define Lil & Jasper's personality.

4. Would we be friends with this brand?
We think so. Lil & Jasper's feels laid-back and happy doing what it's doing. We can't imagine the brand being bossy or faddy about food. We don't get the feeling that it's going to lecture us about salt intake. It's just going to prepare good stuff and let us make our choices.

5. If we wrote a lonely hearts ad for Lil & Jasper's, what would it say?
Genuine and honest individual, early 30s, into grass roots music, home cooking, design and world affairs. Looking for laid-back soul mate to share passions, adventure and travel.

They're only five questions, but they make you really, really think about the personality of your brand or organisation. And it doesn't matter if the brand you're working with is an accountancy practice, a sports center or a manufacturer of motor components – these questions will remain relevant.

They'll help you get to the bottom of who your brand is and what kind of language it should be using.

It can help to boil your answers down to two, three or four words.

For Lil & Jasper's, those words would be:

Laid-back,
Optimistic
and
Happy

RELATIONSHIP *with* AUDIENCES

Every brand or organisation has a defined relationship with its audiences. At Wordtree, we find it helpful to think in terms of the relationships decribed by transactional analysis.

Which is just a fancy way of saying we all fall into different kinds of relationships with different people. In transactional analysis, relationships are defined as being adult, parent or child.

In a **parent-child relationship**, the parent protects and looks after the child. And the child takes little responsibility. If a brand took the role of a parent to a child audience, it would essentially be saying, "Don't you worry about a thing. We'll take care of absolutely everything. We're the experts and we'll look after this." So this could be an appropriate relationship for a luxury holiday brand to have with its consumers. Or maybe a road-side rescue service. It's a tricky relationship for brands though, because no-one likes to be patronised – which is what relationships like this can easily fall into.

In a **child-parent situation**, the brand would need to be the one that was looked after by its consumers. The unspoken dialogue would be, "As a brand, I can't survive if you don't care for me." Which makes it an unlikely model for a successful commercial relationship. Interestingly, some brands that overdo their customer service messaging can stray into this kind of relationship accidentally. Overly subservient messaging can end up sounding like it's seeking approval and forgiveness.

Child-child is an interesting relationship, and in these recessional times it appears to be falling out of favour a little. In this, the brand says, "Oi! You! Let's go play together. I'm in charge! You're it! Ha ha ha!" The brand is inviting you to indulge your inner child and to come and be silly with it. Some lads mags do this. So do a number of food and drink products.

Adult-adult is the kind of relationship that most brands are trying to maintain. It's where the brand is a grown-up, and you're assuming its consumers are too. This is a relationship of equals where no-one gets talked down to or fawned over.

So what relationship does Lil & Jasper's have with its consumers?
Lil & Jasper's has an **adult-adult** relationship with its customers. It's an enthusiastic, but generally laid-back friend that's fun to hang out with. It doesn't bang on about healthy eating – and it would join you for a beer or a glass of wine if you were offering.

Over to you >>>

DEFINING YOUR BRAND'S PERSONALITY

So now it's your turn. Start to think of your brand or organisation as a person. Try to see the brand as other people see it. What is it like? How does it dress? Let's ask some questions.

1. What kind of clothes would your brand wear?

_____

_____

_____

_____

_____

> **Tip**
> If it helps, cut ideas out of a magazine and make a collage.
> Anything that helps you to visualise the brand you're working
> with as a person will help you to create a solid, consistent tone
> of voice.

2. What does your brand do in its spare time?

_____

_____

_____

_____

_____

3. Which newspapers does your brand read? What kind of movies or TV does it like to watch?

_____

_____

_____

_____

_____

4. Would you be friends with your brand? If so, why? If not, what kind of relationship would you have with it?

_____

_____

_____

_____

_____

5. Write a lonely hearts ad for your brand.

_____

_____

_____

_____

_____

6. Now sum up the personality of your brand into a handful of words. Don't use more than four, because this will keep you focussed and accurate.

1. _____

2. _____

3. _____

4. _____

7. What kind of a relationship does your brand want to have with its audiences?

_____

_____

_____

_____

_____

So now you've nailed the personality of your brand, let's give it a voice to match.   > > >

Tip

If you're very close to a brand and you know the people who own it or manage it, try your best not to get caught up in their personalities. While it's inevitable that a smaller organisation will reflect the character of its owner (the whole of the Wordtree team is nodding vigorously at this point), a successful brand will take on a life of its own. So describe the brand, not the owner.

If you're working with a brand you don't know very well yet, then get researching. Find out everything you can about the way it works, its history and its attitudes towards customers. From the last chapter, you know who its competitors are. Now you need to get to know the brand you're working with, inside out.

PAINTING PERSONALITY WITH WORDS

PAINTING PERSONALITY *with* WORDS

PAINTING PERSONALITY *with* WORDS

So far you've learned how to make your writing good and commercial. You've mapped out where your brand sits in its marketplace and you've defined its personality.

Now this is the really fun bit. Remember that thing about language being like clay? Well now it's time to craft it into the shape that perfectly expresses your brand's personality.

This is where you take your good commercial writing skills and overlay them with techniques to convey different personality traits.

We're going to look at how we need to treat language to convey a handful of different personality characteristics. The list isn't comprehensive – but it will give you a good overview of some of the styles of writing we're often asked to produce at Wordtree.

ENERGY *and* PACE v. RELAXING *and* RESTFUL

If your brand wants to be perceived as a go-getting, can-do kind of organisation, it's a good idea to get some energy into its tone of voice.

Short words and sentences, as well as sentence fragments, are really your friends here. You want the reader to gallop through your messages with ease. This will give them the impression that your organisation deals with things efficiently and simply.

Used sparingly, alliteration of harder sounds can also help to convey pace. This is where you have similar consonant sounds following one another like *boil in the bag* or *click and connect.*

If, however, you want to convey leisure and a kind of luxurious floaty feeling, go in the opposite direction. Your sentences can become longer (though not so long that you can't read them out loud in one breath). You can also carefully select some longer words to use.

The sounds that help to convey leisure, relaxation and a completely chilled and languid personality are soft – so try using sibilance in your writing. This means repeating sounds like sh, suh, zzz and sss.

Consonance, where a consonant sound is repeated anywhere in the words, gives a softer, lilting quality to text.

After everything, laughter will never fail.

Consonance can be a useful tool to convey peacefulness.

EXAMPLE

THE BRIEF	ENERGY *and* PACE	RELAXING, RESTFUL *and* LEISURELY
Tell our customers about our new cookie range. **Key messages:** • Textured and tasty • Large pieces of real milk chocolate	Crunchy, crumbly cookies crammed with chunky chocolate chips. Yum.	From the first sweet and succulent mouthful you'll be lost in a delicious swirl of chocolate heaven.
	This feels fun, easy and a bit of a romp. Note though, it's hard for writing that rattles out the information like this to feel premium.	This is a slower read and the effect is to make the message feel more relaxed. The sibilant "s" sounds are calming. The same message is made to feel like a more decadent, more premium experience.

WHIMSICAL

Whimsy is a personality trait you either love or hate in writing. To convey a whimsical personality you've got to dig out your inner child and see the world through his or her eyes.

Which means using the expressions a child might – so keep the words simple and the sentences short. Using contractions is a given. And starting sentences with conjunctions works well too.

Personification is an easy way to convey a whimsical personality. It doesn't matter if you're writing about cheese or gardening tools, if you stop treating them like inanimate objects and allow them to magically come to life and speak to your reader, you're well on the road to whimsy.

But there has to be naïvety and innocence, because whimsy is polite and wholesome. If your writing seems in the least bit knowing, it will transform into something teasing and sexually suggestive.

Another word of caution with whimsy. It's not one of those styles you can just dip your toe into. If you're going to do it, you've got to really do it. Otherwise you'll feel embarrassed and your reader will too.

And remember, resist the urge to use exclamation marks. Your writing should be strong enough without them – and if it isn't, they won't help anyway.

EXAMPLE

THE BRIEF	Oooh, you chose Florida Blue. Let's go and write some lovely letters that feel like the sea. Or maybe a book – yes, let's write a book together.
Our writing inks have been on the market for years, but we're aware people are now buying more fountain pens, and we want to appeal to a younger audience. We don't want to be seen as a fuddy-duddy old ink company, so please make us feel accessible and quirky. We just need a few words for the back of pack.	It's polite, it's child-like and the person who bought the ink will either be completely tickled or they'll throw the packaging away in disgust.

Be careful. This is what happens to whimsy if you take the naïvety out of it. Whimsy minus the innocence leads to something altogether more suggestive.

EXAMPLE

THE BRIEF	Oooh, you chose spicy orange and cinnamon cream. Slide me sensuously out of this wrapper. Lick me. Bite me. Devour me.
Our chocolate bars have grown-up flavours and we want them to appeal to adults via a cheeky sense of humour. **Key message:** • The sensuousness of our flavours • These chocolates are for grown-ups	If a computer were to analyse the ink paragraph and the spicy orange chocolate paragraph, it wouldn't find a huge amount of difference, because syntactically they're almost identical. But the ink personality is naïve, and the orange chocolate one just isn't.

Tip

There's a very, very fine line between playful childishness and flirty adult communication. If you need to convey the former for your brand, make sure you'd be happy for a six-year-old to read everything you've written.

SCIENTIFIC

Conveying a scientific personality is all about feeling efficient and authoritative. Both of these call for short words and short-ish sentences.

It wouldn't be unreasonable to think that to convey a scientific tone in a commercial environment, you'd need to write something akin to a scientific report. But please don't do that, because scientific reports go against all the rules for good commercial writing.

Instead, to make your reader feel the white coat and lab equipment, write the words and phrases you'd imagine a brisk army sergeant major would use. Talk in terms of operations, missions, combat and encounters.

It helps to reduce your use of contractions too, as this will make the text feel slightly cooler and more clipped and dispassionate.

Some brands like to use neologisms to convey "science". This is where you just make a word up, so you get things like: *Only Brand X comes with Proviva Sani-vac® technology.* At Wordtree, we're not great fans of pseudo scientific words. We think they can sound like you're trying to pull the wool over your reader's eyes.

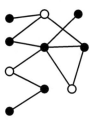

EXAMPLE

THE BRIEF	**Brand X** Operation safe home
Brand X is used by hospitals because it eliminates all known forms of harmful gastric bacteria. We're now launching it on the domestic market. **Key consumer insight:** • Carers in households fear their loved ones becoming ill – especially through inefficient cleaning **Key message:** • Bring laboratory-grade technology into your home	Formulated to combat the most aggressive bacteria, Brand X brings laboratory-grade technology into your home. With Brand X as your first line of defence, your family will enjoy ultimate protection. Zero tolerance on bacteria. Mission accomplished.
	This conveys a completely no-nonsense, functional tone. It's the kind of tone you might want to use if you want to position a brand as a life-and-death necessity rather than a lifestyle choice.

Tip

A "scientific" voice is often called for by pharmaceutical and some cosmetic brands. Cleaning products are an obvious candidate too. A brisk, militaristic use of language will help your readers to feel the science and efficiency.

DEGREES *of* FRIENDLINESS

There are very few brands that don't want to appear friendly – or at least "accessible".

And this isn't surprising. We live in a society where the boundaries are ever-shifting and consumers largely expect to have relationships with brands that are based on equality.

But there are different ways of interacting in a friendly way. One of the concerns we often hear about tone of voice from our corporate clients is a fear that we're going to "dumb down". Often, this really means there's anxiety that we'll introduce language that makes the conversation not just friendly, but downright informal – perhaps inappropriately so.

One of the most useful definitions of the word "friendly" that we use at Wordtree is:

• Favourably disposed; not antagonistic

It's a good starting point for our spectrum of friendliness. Because being favourably disposed doesn't exclude professionalism – or even a degree of formality.

From there, we can move into other shades of friendly – through a less-guarded friendliness, all the way to over-familiarity and matiness.

Where your brand needs to be on the spectrum of friendliness will be defined by its personality and the kind of relationships it wants to have with consumers.

PROFESSIONALLY FRIENDLY

People who recoil at the thought of their commercial writing being described as "friendly" would usually be equally horrified at the thought of any of their clients being treated discourteously.

Their fear about "friendly" is that it might go too far and become over-familiar. But professional friendliness doesn't have to be sentimental or intrusive. It can just be a matter of making the language quick and easy to read, not being afraid of using contractions, and using shorter words.

If a brand has a friendly personality, it should also use personal pronouns and avoid using the passive voice:

You're very welcome to visit us.

Rather than

Vistors are made very welcome at the Brand X establishment.

In other words, professionally friendly language is pretty much the starting point for all good commercial writing. It's open, easy to get along with and feels honest.

UNGUARDED FRIENDLINESS

To turn the warmth up a notch, we can introduce more contractions and let the language relax slightly to include more of the words and phrases we'd happily use when we're speaking, but are sometimes less inclined to write down.

OVER-FAMILIAR *and* MATEY

For the right kind of brand, this can be an effective tone, but it's only really advisable when your brand's proposition is about shared experience rather than expertise.

So a matey tone might work really well for a deodorant that claims to boost your attractiveness. Or for a lads' magazine. If your brand uses this tone, then decorum shouldn't have much of a role to play in the relationship it wants to have with its consumers.

EXAMPLE

UNFRIENDLY	PROFESSIONALLY FRIENDLY	UNGUARDED FRIENDLINESS	MATINESS/ OVER-FAMILIARITY
Free product marketing sample. Feedback can be posted on Facebook.	Please enjoy this free sample of our new chocolate bar. If you'd like to tell us what you think of it, please visit us on Facebook.	We thought you'd like a free sample of our new choccie bars. We love them. Hope you do too. Tell us what you think about them on Facebook.	Oi cheeky chops! These new choccie bars are amazing. Get a load of them down your neck and don't blame us if you get toothache. Tell the world how great they are on Facebook.
There is no warmth in this statement. It is all about the brand and has nothing at all to do with the consumer and the brand's relationship with them. It's completely devoid of emotion – part due to the lack of personal pronouns and the use of the passive voice.	This is unsentimental and straightforward. It also feels open and honest because it uses easy words and short sentences. It's perfectly pleasant, without trying to cosy up to the reader.	A warmer relationship is intimated in these words. It gives the reader a very clear idea of the brand's personality and the close and chummy relationship it wants to have with its consumers. The extra warmth is achieved using more vernacular language and sentence fragments. This makes the text feel less guarded and more at ease in the company of the reader.	This is an in-your-face way of conveying the same information. It has crossed the line from straightforward dialogue into banter. It's packed with vernacular and it has a slight arrogance to it. To readers, it can come across as either highly entertaining or offensive – so think carefully before you decide this kind of friendliness is right for your brand.

Tip
"Friendly" and "professional" are not mutually exclusive.
Don't repel your readers with complexity and stuffiness
just because you're trying to avoid over-familiarity.

DOWN-*to*-EARTH v. POSH

People can become very uncomfortable when you start to talk about links between language and social class.

People might be happy using the word "posh" if they're talking about crisps. But they don't like saying, "Look, this upholstery business I run, well I want it to sound jolly posh." They'll talk all around the houses about a "premium service" based on traditional values.

In reality, there's little doubt that language can express social class, but we do understand the nervousness. No-one wants to appear a snob.

But the word "premium" could be interpreted in so many different ways. So for the sake of example, we've stuck with the word "posh".

Down-to-earth commercial language is achieved by using all the things we use when we talk – contractions, idiom, short words and sentence fragments.

If you think posh commercial language might move in completely the opposite direction, then you may be surprised. Structurally, there's actually very little difference between posh language and down-to-earth language.

The only thing you need to elevate posh commercial language is carefully chosen vocabulary. So instead of choosing a short, sharp Anglo-Saxon word, you might allow yourself a Latinate word instead. The underlying sentence structure is exactly the same as down-to-earth.

The trick is not to overdo it with the longer words. You don't want to create text that's heavy with Latinate vocabulary, or you'll just end up conveying a stuffy old bore of a personality. Instead, hand pick a beautiful Latinate word and place it very carefully into the sentence. It should shine out like a sophisticated jewel in a subtle setting.

EXAMPLE

DOWN-TO-EARTH	POSH
With ladies and men's watches from all the top brands along with charm bracelets and other dazzling jewellery, we've got glitz and glamour galore.	Whether you're selecting a classic timepiece or something sparkling and special, we have a delightful range for you to choose from.

> *Tip*
> Hard alliteration – *glitz and glamour galore* – rarely sounds premium, but consonance and sibilance really can – *selecting a classic, something sparkling and special.*

RETRO VOICES

There are trends in language, just as there are in design. As we've been writing this book, the UK is still fondly remembering a royal wedding and memorabilia from the Queen's Diamond Jubilee is still in the shops. That coupled with one of the worst recessions in living memory means that retro has been pretty popular.

But again, there are different types of retro. We're going to look at two of the most popular – Dickensian retro and 1950s retro.

A Dickensian style of language can be appropriate for a food brand that wants to convey heritage or old-fashioned values. It can feel quaint and make a brand feel reassuringly established.

To achieve it, you need to allow yourself to wallow in slightly lengthier sentences that use Latinate and archaic vocabulary. But as always, don't forget the rules of good commercial writing. Dickensian retro might be challenging for you to write, but it should never be difficult to read.

RETRO VOICES

Retro, particularly from the 1950s, is interesting and a lot of fun to write. It has a superbly wholesome feel. And to achieve it, it helps to imagine that you're writing in the voice of Enid Blyton. It has a naïve and unworldly quality to it as well, which can make it perfect for a brand that wants to convey that it's an all-round good egg that doesn't get mixed up in sophisticated nonsense.

If you're writing in a 1950s style, you could do far worse than spend an afternoon reading a Famous Five book. If you don't have time for such leisurely activity, there are a handful of words and phrases that, carefully deployed, will immediately whisk your reader off to a world of sunlit bicycle rides and lashings of ginger beer. These include: scrumptious, jolly, crikey, parlour, supper, I daresay and delightful. Don't overdo it though, or it will sound like satire.

EXAMPLE

MODERN	1950s	DICKENSIAN
Carruthers' crisps Perfect with a light lunch, or just on their own for a treat.	*Carruthers' crisps* Well, if we do say it ourselves Carruthers makes jolly nice crisps. They pack a perfectly piquant punch, and make an ideal accompaniment to a good ham sandwich.	*Carruthers' potato chips* Our founder Jeremiah Carruthers held a firm belief that a gentleman of good standing should never be in want of a hearty bite to eat. Indeed, his travelling case had a special compartment for these deliciously substantial potato chips.

Tip
Retro writing can be quite difficult to pull off, and it can look amateur if you don't quite get it right. Take your time when you're writing retro. Immerse yourself in the language of the period – but remember the rules of good commercial writing.

A WORD *on* CONVEYING NATIONALITY

Provenance is often very important, and can form a significant part of a brand's identity.

Swiss jewellers often communicate in efficient, engineering-type writing styles that describe pens as "writing instruments" and watches as "timepieces". Distilleries often introduce a hint of location into their communications.

In tone of voice, evoking nationality means making teeny adjustments to things like word order and vocabulary. These subliminal linguistic cues can be highly effective.

A brand like Jack Daniel's, doesn't have to tell you it's from the South of the USA – you can just hear it in the politeness of the words, the slightly lengthier sentences and the story telling. They're words that make you feel like you need to draw up a chair and settle down for a while, because the world of the author isn't one where information is rattled out in a hurry.

A WORD *on* CONVEYING NATIONALITY

Meanwhile Hermes, the French luxury brand, uses word order and the odd French word to convey its nationality in English language communications. Their description of a scarf, for example, uses the phrase "we pay him tribute" instead of "we pay tribute to him" – and uses the word "enfant" instead of "child". Which is just enough to make it feel very French indeed.

To evoke nationality, listen to native speakers talking in English. YouTube is a great resource – so are local newspapers and blogs. Take note of their word order and any unusual vocabulary.

Word order is a really easy and effective way of communicating nationality. Vocabulary can be, but only if it's understood widely enough for it not to be confusing.

When you've pinpointed a couple of devices, weave them gently into your writing.

EXAMPLE

PROVENANCE UNCLEAR	LIKELY TO BE FRENCH	LIKELY TO BE AMERICAN
Tiny lemon chocolates	*Petits chocolats au citron*	*Mini lemon delights*
A whisper of citrus wrapped up in a whirl of white chocolate mousse. The perfect gift.	A suspicion of citrus wrapped in delicious mousse au chocolat blanc. Make a gift of them.	If life hands you lemons, just wrap 'em up in white chocolate. The perfect gift for someone you love.

> **Tip**
> Evoke nationality with care. The idea isn't to create caricatures.
> It should be about reinforcing the authenticity of your brand
> with carefully crafted writing.

A NOTE *on* LESS DESIRABLE PERSONALITY TRAITS

Few brands will deliberately convey a personality that's pompous, indecisive, woolly or lacking in confidence. Yet many do it unintentionally.

It usually goes back to good commercial writing being a world away from academic writing. Styles of writing and communicating that guarantee high marks in university can bomb in a commercial environment.

Long sentences can sound waffly and unsure. In a commercial setting, they can convey a lack of confidence. This is completely the opposite of writing for a university tutor, who might be moved to award top marks to the intellect that can string long, obscure words together in complex sentences.

But think about it. Your university tutors were doing a job they loved – pondering the realms of complexity and gauging the impressions they'd made on young, intelligent minds.

But in a commercial environment, your reader doesn't really want to read what you've written, and they are not approaching the task with joy. No-one but no-one gets a brochure about pensions and thinks, "Ah, brilliant. I've got a nice bottle of Rioja in the pantry, and now I've got this to read. Never mind the TV or going out – I've got my night sorted now."

No. What they're thinking is, "Oh man, this had better be simple."

Overly complicated language – long words and complex grammatical constructions – can also convey a lack of confidence.

While the author might be thinking, "Ha! Just check out my knowledge of long words and complex grammar and how intelligent that makes me look," the effect on the reader can be quite the opposite.

Monster sentences and big slabs of words can make it sound like the author is hiding behind the words. It feels like they don't know their subject well enough to just say it simply.

So don't show off with the words. Don't think you have to be clever. Because to a reader who's less than enthusiastic anyway, you'll end up sounding pompous and ineffectual.

A WORD *on* STAYING POSITIVE

No brand or organisation wants to sound negative. In fact, business speak has created so many euphemisms for negative concepts, a visitor from the past might think nothing bad ever happens in modern business.

Actually, a visitor from the past would probably have no idea at all about what is being said in modern business, but that's besides this point.

A style of writing can certainly enhance positivity by introducing pace (if your brand's take on positivity is to get things done, chop-chop). Or it can evoke a feeling of relaxation and happy calm.

But to really be positive, you've got to think about framing messages in a more upbeat way.

So many companies communicate in terms of what they're not and what they don't do. The aim of this is usually to spell out that they're not like all the other companies – that they do things better and differently.

But the negative spin is usually a mistake, and it can come across as curmudgeonly, or even smug.

It's all because written communications make all kinds of pictures fire up in your readers' brains. So if you write:

There was a large tree in the middle of the field.

Everyone who reads the sentence, no matter where in the world they live, how old they are or what political views they have, will imagine some kind of field with some kind of large tree in it.

And our brains work pretty quickly. Before your readers have even got to the field bit, they're already feeling the green of the tree and maybe even remembering what gnarled bark feels like to run the palm of your hand against.

So if you frame messages in the negative, you're just evoking negative thoughts in your reader – or at least putting them on their guard that negativity is coming their way. So be careful with it.

Framing your messages in a more consistently positive way will have a big impact on the tonality of your whole style of writing.

EXAMPLE

NEGATIVE FRAMING	POSITIVE FRAMING
We don't just get your packages to you quickly, we guarantee they'll arrive next day.	We guarantee your package will arrive next day.
We are concerned not only with short-term achievements, but also with sustainable development over the long term.	We build for the long term, celebrating achievements along the way.
Fairy Cupcakes Inc isn't a bakery. We don't just make cakes. We make sugar-spun dreams and we create recipes for happiness.	This is where dreams are spun from sugar. This is where we pour sunshine into recipes and wrap mouthwatering happiness in ribbons. This is Fairy Cupcakes Inc.

Tip

If you see words like "don't" and "not only" appearing on your page, stop. Think how you might frame your message in a positive way and try that instead. Remember to read what you've written out loud to hear how it sounds to the reader.

COMBINING TRAITS

There will be brands that only need to adopt one of the styles set out in this chapter. More commonly, though, a brand's personality will have a number of different characteristics.

If we think, for example, of a shampoo brand that wants to convey science and friendliness, then it would have some combining to do.

We know that to convey a scientific personality, we need to imagine the words that an army major would use. Friendliness, however, allows us to relax and use contractions and vernacular.

Individually, neither a scientific nor a friendly voice are right. Blended, they create an appropriate tone.

EXAMPLE

SCIENTIFIC	FRIENDLY	BLENDED
Luscious Loxx shampoo's targeted action bonds split follicles to boost shininess by up to 80%.	Luscious Loxx shampoo makes your hair super shiny – and its sophisticated fragrance will make you feel a real glamourpuss.	The targeted action of Luscious Loxx will bond any pesky split ends, making your hair up to 80% shinier. Oh, and it smells fantastic too.

SO HOW CAN WE USE THIS INFORMATION *to* CREATE A TONE *of* VOICE FOR LIL & JASPER'S?

We've already defined the personality of our invented healthy frozen pizza brand, Lil & Jasper's. We described it as:

Laid-back,
Optimistic
and
Happy

We know that each of these personality traits can be conveyed with a certain use of words.

Laid-back

We know our sentences can become longer to give a feeling of pleasurable meandering. But we're not trying to sound luxuriously laid-back, so we'll probably stick with shorter words. We may also use sibilant sounds to help us convey contentment and relaxation.

Optimistic and happy

We need to remember to frame our messages positively.

Lil & Jasper's tone of voice

This gives us the backbone of the tone for Lil & Jasper's personality. We know that we'll be using mostly shorter words, but not super-short sentences. We know that we'll be keeping messages positive.

We also know that Lil & Jasper's is an American brand. So we'll be looking to introduce tiny pieces of vocabulary and word order that give readers subliminal clues about where this tasty pizza comes from.

EXAMPLES

ABOUT US PAGE OF LIL & JASPER'S WEBSITE	COMMENTS
Lil and I have always had a thing for good food – you know, nothing too structured, just wholesome, organic, great-tasting stuff.	The sentences are at the longer end of what works in a commercial setting. This gives them a slow, contended, leisurely feel – but they're not too long because you can read them out loud in one breath.
When we opened the deli, we thought of it like an extension of our home. A lot of our customers were our friends, and new customers became our friends. I guess everyone just kinda likes that we don't hurry them along.	"I guess" and "kinda" and "be sure to visit" are phrases more associated with American English speakers.
Anyway, we open up early for lunch and stay up late for the night crowd Then we started to think that we should box up meals to go.	The delivery is unhurried, and the reader feels they're dealing with someone who's upbeat and on their side.
Because we love it when customers can come in and spend time with us. But we want to make sure they've got good food, even when they're on the run.	
And when you do get time to drop by, me and Lil will be thrilled to share our latest food finds with you. Be sure to visit.	

INTRODUCTION LETTER

Dear Waitrose,

We've got a new range of frozen pizzas we'd like to come and show you all.

Lil & Jasper's pizzas have been literally life changing for tens of thousands of west coast Americans – and they've been just so popular at the farmers' markets, we've taken them to the UK.

It's because they're convenient and healthy. And while we'd love for all our customers to come visit us in the Lil & Jasper's deli, we know people just don't always have the time.

But it makes us happy to think that there's a slice of Lil & Jasper's just waiting in the freezer any time a person wants good food on the go.

So can we come show them to you? Or would you like to drop by the deli?

We hope to hear from you soon,

Lil & Jasper's

EXERCISES

1. Jot down the words that describe the personality of your brand.

_____

_____

_____

2. Select the styles you will need to combine to paint your brand's personality.
Go through the styles of writing described in this chapter and identify the ones that are going to best help you to paint the personality of your brand. List them, and make notes what about each style makes the words do.

_____

_____

_____

_____

_____

EXERCISES

3. What will characterise the way your brand uses language? Short sentences? Sentence fragments? Short words? Long words? Consonance?

---

4. Play with your words.

Take two important pieces of text for your brand – maybe the about us page of your website or a letter of introduction – and write them in the new tone.

Don't forget to make sure you're using all the rules of good commercial writing as a starting point. And don't be afraid to really push it. You're only going to get comfortable with a new tone of voice by playing with it until it's exactly right.

Read them out loud to get a better feel for what they sound like to the reader.

5. Get into tone.

To get to grips with the mechanics of tonality, it can be really helpful to listen to a person speaking and think very carefully about what you're inferring about their character from their words.

Radio is a great way to do this, because you're not distracted by the way someone looks or is dressed.

Jot down some notes about what kind of a person you think you're listening to.

_____

_____

_____

_____

_____

_____

It's helpful to write down word for word what the person has said. Then you can look at the exact words and begin to analyse why they've given you the impression they have.

USE A CHECKLIST

- Do I find this person interesting?
- Am I having trouble following what they're saying?
- Do I care about what they're saying?
- Is this person energetic?
- Are they confident or flustered?
- Do they sound like they know what they're talking about?
- Do they sound slippery?
- Are they being honest?
- Do they sound relevant and modern?

You may be surprised at how certain types of vocabulary, lengths of sentences and sentence constructions actually make you feel. And it's all great insight into how your words will make your audiences feel.

And if you hear someone whose words make you feel inspired, motivated and well disposed towards them, make sure you jot everything down and replicate their speech patterns in your own commercial writing.

Similarly, if someone's words make you feel depressed or angry – take notes, and be sure to avoid however they're using language.

We can almost hear what you're thinking right now, "This is all well and good, but no-one speaks the same way all the time, surely?" Absolutely right. So let's go and find out about

VOLUME CONTROL

VOLUME CONTROL

VOLUME CONTROL

What we've been looking at all the way through this book is expressing brand personality in words. That's what tone of voice is all about.

And we've looked at how different personality traits can be conveyed with certain writing devices.

But in real life, no personality is ever expressed in the same way all the time.

Healthy human beings learn very quickly how to moderate their personalities for different occasions.

So if we're at a funeral, or a job interview – or if we ever have to give evidence in court – we're going to be our my most polite, reserved settings of ourselves.

But when we go about our daily business – maybe taking part in meetings or going to the shops – then our personalities come out on a "louder", more relaxed setting.

And if we're celebrating with friends and family – maybe a couple of glasses of rosé into the night – our personality is most likely to be out at full strength.

This is a really important part of human interaction. If we didn't have the ability to do polite and reserved, we'd probably be unemployable. But if we could only do polite and reserved, we probably wouldn't be invited to many parties.

The crucial thing in all of this is that we don't change who we are in these different circumstances – we just let our personalities out at lower or higher volumes.

It's important for any brand voice to have this flexibility too.

Because even a friendly and fun brand has to have the ability to write a condolence letter that won't offend. And the most authoritative and technical brand has to be able to advertise and celebrate in a way that won't put people to sleep.

HOW HIGH *is* HIGH?

HOW LOW *is* LOW?

"Oooh, I'm so deliciously squidgy!"

One of the things that puts some people off the thought of tone of voice is that they've seen how high the volume of some brands can go.

If your brand sits in an inherently conservative sector – for example, finance or legal – you may shudder at the thought of the, "Oooh, I'm so deliciously squidgy!" tone of say, a chocolate pudding brand.

And quite right too.

Each brand has its own parameters. High volume for your brand may mean displaying very high levels of intelligent word play.

And if you're in a completely different sector it might even mean using text speak and made up words.

It all depends on the personality of your brand.

VOLUME CONTROL *in* ACTION

Let's see how volume control works with our healthy pizza brand Lil & Jasper's tone of voice.

First of all, we've got to decide what kind of communication will fall into which volume setting.

Some are really easy. If we're writing a letter of condolence, or chasing up a bad debt, that feels like it should be polite and reserved. In other words, low volume.

If we're writing happy, celebratory or advertising material, that feels higher volume.

LIL & JASPER'S VOLUME CONTROL

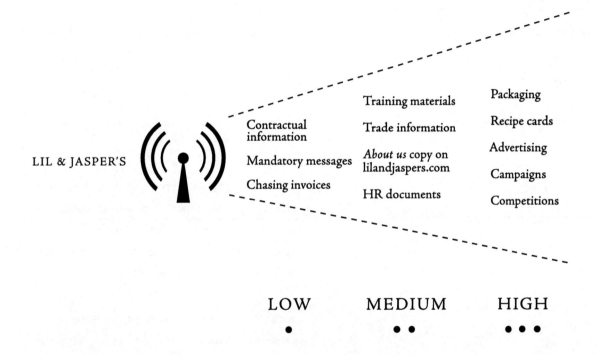

LIL & JASPER'S

Contractual information

Mandatory messages

Chasing invoices

Training materials

Trade information

About us copy on lilandjaspers.com

HR documents

Packaging

Recipe cards

Advertising

Campaigns

Competitions

LOW
•

MEDIUM
• •

HIGH
• • •

•

Then you need to think about the adaptations you need to make to your tone to turn the volume up or down. The important thing is not to change the personality of your brand just because you're writing at different volume levels. Remember, it's the same personality, just reacting to different circumstances.

In real life, one of the things we all tend to do when we're being polite and reserved is to talk more slowly. You can give the impression of this in your writing by having slightly longer sentences than you might normally have – but don't break any of the rules of good writing and make them so long that you can't read your sentences out loud in one breath.

Another thing we all tend to do in low volume circumstances is pronounce our words more carefully. So it may be appropriate for you to use fewer contractions at low volume to mimic this.

Readers are likely to need to pay greater attention to low volume copy, so make sure it's clear and straightforward to follow.

MEDIUM VOLUME

• •

As the circumstances become less serious, we begin to relax a little. We might become more playful with the words we're using – and we'll probably use more contractions.

We'll also be looking for the text to pick up the pace, so we can begin to really get some rhythm and speed into the words.

HIGH VOLUME

• • •

This is when our words are all dressed up for a big night out.

In linguistic terms we can be a bit more showy. If your brand allows for very high volume, it can be the equivalent of wearing a feather headdress and slapping on the glitter.

If your brand is inherently a bit more serious and calm, it can be like putting on a bright silk tie and tucking a matching hankie into your top pocket.

Because at high volume, you get to use the little flourishes that can make commercial writing really fun.

Over the page, we'll see how those adaptations work for Lil & Jasper's.

>>>

LIL & JASPER'S VOLUME CONTROL

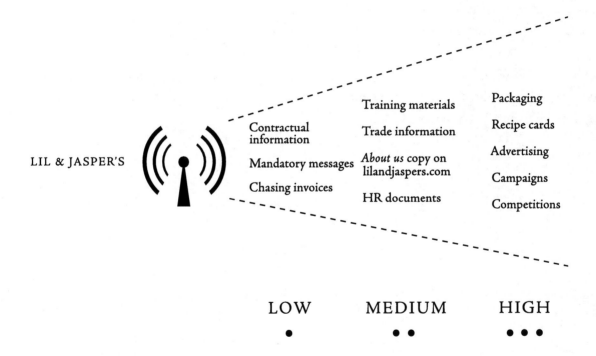

LIL & JASPER'S

Contractual information

Mandatory messages

Chasing invoices

Training materials

Trade information

About us copy on lilandjaspers.com

HR documents

Packaging

Recipe cards

Advertising

Campaigns

Competitions

LOW •

MEDIUM • •

HIGH • • •

LOW

•

Our sentences are at the longer end of what works well in commercial writing.

We use contractions sparingly and we're less likely to start sentences with conjunctions.

Word order and punctuation is American.

MEDIUM

• •

The language starts to relax a little more.

We begin to start sentences with conjunctions and more vernacular starts to creep in.

We also use contractions more freely.

HIGH

• • •

The personality really shines through now.

We play with the language, making maximum use of sibillance and consonance.

The pace is unhurried, but we keep it fresh with simple syntax and vocabulary.

EXAMPLES ••• HIGH

See your creation become the next Lil & Jasper's pizza

You guys know what we're all about here at Lil & Jasper's – good food that keeps you healthy even when life's on full throttle.

Well here's our idea. We'd love for you to send us your ideas for a totally new Lil & Jasper's pizza. We're looking for deliciousness that will perk up the busiest person when they take it out of their freezer.

Tell us about your local ingredients, tell us what makes your mouth water. And who knows? By this time next year, hundreds of thousands of folk could be enjoying your creation.

Email your recipe to topthis@lilandjaspers.com. Be sure to include your name, address and mobile telephone number. For the small print, just visit our website.

Good luck. We can't wait to see what you create.

EXAMPLES • • MEDIUM

Letter to a supplier

Hi guys,
Just to let you know, it's competition time at Lil & Jasper's.

We're asking all our lovely Lil & Jasper's people in the UK to create a new pizza for the range. They can email their ideas to us and when we've picked a winner we'll put their pizza into production and they'll become famous all over the pizza-eating world.

So look out for our new competition packs, and if you've got a great idea for a deliciously healthy pizza, be sure to let us know.

Thanks to you all,
Lil & Jasper's

EXAMPLES • LOW

The Lil & Jasper's Create A Pizza competition rules

Who can enter?
Anyone who lives in the UK, and who's already had their sixteenth birthday.

Who can't?
Anyone who works for us, and everyone they're related to. Sorry guys, that's what we pay you for.

How do you enter?
Just email your recipe to us, along with your name and mobile telephone number.

How many times can you enter?
Only once – so be sure to make it count.

When are we picking a winner?
On Sunday, November 25, 2012. Then the new pizza will start to be hand made in January 2013.

Good luck, guys – and thanks for taking time to enter.

A WORD *on* AUDIENCES

In workshops people often ask if volume control changes depending on the audience.

Our answer is simply, no.

Your personality doesn't change when you talk to different people. All that happens is that when you speak in more formal and serious circumstances, you reign your personality in a little.

And when you speak in less formal circumstances, you allow your personality out more.

You change volume because of circumstances, not audiences.

"No."

A WORD *on* VOLUME

Interestingly, low volume is often where tone of voice goes out of the window – even for some of the world's most well-known and respected brands.

We often see it happening because a lot of low volume content is uncomfortable to write. And when writers feel uncomfortable, they can take refuge in a highly impersonal, overly formal and bureaucratic style that says, "Look, it's not me that's writing this, it's a faceless organisation. Please don't blame me, it's just the rules."

But it's an approach that doesn't help the reader much – and it certainly doesn't help to differentiate your brand.

Writing in a consistent brand voice at low volume takes courage.

So take a deep breath and be true to your brand's personality.

EXAMPLE

Dear Mr Smith, It has come to our attention that the aforementioned invoice remains unpaid by ACME Industries Plc, despite two previous attempts at reclamation. In these circumstances there is little option but to seek legal redress via the courts and their offices. Please note that should payment not be forthcoming within seven days of the date on this correspondence, our solicitors Payup, Grabbit & Winnit will pursue payment via the courts. If you have made payment while this correspondence was in transit, please ignore this letter. Kind regards, Lil & Jasper's	Dear Mr Smith, We still haven't received your payment for this invoice. We now have to advise you that you have seven days from the date on this letter to settle the invoice – or we will have to go to court. We'd much rather you just paid it though. We're right here if you want to contact us. Best wishes, Lil & Jasper's

EXERCISES

1. Make a list of all the communications you generate.
Don't forget all the little bits and pieces like price tickets, menus, letters to clients and customers, and automated responses on your website.

Jot your list down here:

_____

_____

_____

_____

_____

_____

2. Your brand's volume control.

Take time deciding where your pieces of communication sit and then jot them down on the diagram below. Some communications are easy to place. With others you may find they straddle medium and high – and that's completely normal. You might want to give these kinds of communications a high volume headline, but keep the body copy to medium volume.

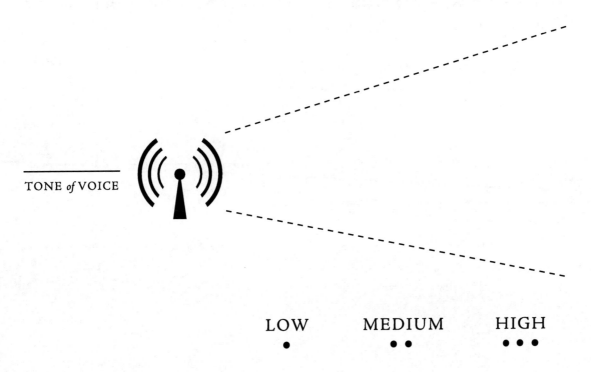

TONE *of* VOICE

LOW   MEDIUM   HIGH

3. How high is high? How low is low?

You've already decided what personality you want to convey with your brand, you've set out your tone of voice and you know which writing devices you're going to use to achieve it. It's important you also decide where the boundaries of high and low volume are for your brand.

Imagine your brand has to attend a sombre occasion. If your brand was a person, how would they dress for this occasion?

Write your description down here:

_____

_____

_____

_____

_____

They're approached by a very serious colleague or friend. How will they talk? Write down their answers to these questions:

Did you find us without any problems?

_____

_____

_____

_____

It's been a long time since we've seen each other, hasn't it?

_____

_____

_____

_____

Write a job advert for a new project manager for your brand.
Don't rush into it. Take this opportunity to experiment with pushing your volume. Because it's only by pushing beyond what you feel comfortable with that you'll find out where your natural level is. It may surprise you.

Now with the same job ad, force the volume to go higher.

Maybe use shorter sentences, maybe use more contractions, and try starting sentences with conjunctions. This could also be an opportunity to use the kinds of phrases we use when we speak. So instead of saying, "Please forward your CV to" you could try using, "Drop us a line at".

_____

_____

_____

_____

_____

_____

We've come to the end of the exercises now – and nearly to the end of the textbook. We've just got a couple of things left to say before you unleash your new tone of voice on the world.

ROUNDUP

ROUNDUP

Tone of voice is still a relatively new discipline, and companies and corporations have only begun to dedicate serious resources to it over the course of the last decade.

But it's taking hold because it works. Considered, crafted language helps organisations to focus more on their customers and to develop long-lasting relationships with them. And that translates into greater success.

This textbook sums up a lot of what we've learned working with some of the world's top brands over the last few years, and sets out the process we use on all our tone of voice projects.

If you're going away to develop a tone of voice for your organisation now, make sure you give yourself plenty of time to research how both your competitors and the brands you admire use language. You might find that you can carve out a distinct and recognisable space for your organisation, simply by using language differently to everyone else in your sector.

Then let yourself play with the words. Remember, you don't have to get it right first time – or second or third time, come to that. The Wordtree team is made up of professional writers and marketers, and our notebooks are full of scribbles, experiments and crossings out. And that's because all the doodling is necessary – it lets you try things out and see if your brilliant spark of an idea stands up in different circumstances.

There's a myth that good writers just knock out great copy because they have some kind of supernatural ability to create. The reality is that good writers get good in the same way that sports people or musicians get good. They may have a grain of talent, but it's the hours and hours of practising that makes their performance seem effortless. And to stay good, you've got to keep practising and learning.

Also, don't let yourself get too hung up on "the rules". Language is an evolving beast – and the English language in particular is a feral beast. It grows and changes on a daily basis. So if you need to bend a few of the rules your English teacher was fond of, it's fine – so long as your communications make immediate and unambiguous sense.

Most importantly, enjoy it. Words are magical and powerful things. They let you take an idea that's in your head and pop it into the minds of readers you'll most likely never even meet. Remember, they're your words and you're in charge of the way they make your readers feel.

If you have ideas or questions about tone of voice – or about your brand – we'd love to hear from you.

We'd love it if you could come to one of our workshops too. You can find out when and where they are on our website – **www.wordtree.com**.